Goodrich Castle

HEREFORDSHIRE

DEREK RENN PhD, FSA

Superbly sited, high above the River Wye, Goodrich Castle was a fortified baronial palace. Its medieval buildings are still largely intact (except for some roofs and floors) and are protected by wide and deep ditches cut into the rock.

A Norman tower stands three storeys high, surrounded by high walls and round drum towers added in the thirteenth and fourteenth centuries. Inside the walls are the remains of three separate halls with attached residential suites ranged round a courtyard. The castle was entered through a strong gatehouse, further protected by an unusual outer defence. The home successively of the families of Marshal, Valence and Talbot, Goodrich Castle was unoccupied by the sixteenth century but was strong enough to withstand a major siege in 1646 during the English Civil War.

This English Heritage Handbook takes you on a tour of the castle (guided by a numbered plan and aerial view), describing it as it is now and as it was when first built. A short history of the castle and those connected with it is also included. The illustration above shows the southeast tower and keep.

English ⊞ Heritage
LONDON

Contents

*Unless otherwise stated illustrations
are copyright English Heritage and
photographs were taken by the
English Heritage Photographic Section*

*Published by English Heritage
23 Savile Row, London W1S 2ET
© Copyright English Heritage 1993
First published 1993, reprinted 1998, 1999, 2002
Printed in England by ABC Printers
C30 05/02 04251
ISBN 1 85074 368 1*

Tour of the Castle

*...ast face of the castle seen across the dry moat from the barbican. The east window of the chapel
... to the left of the entrance*

...he castle stands on a high ridge ...verlooking an old crossing-point of the ...ver. The present approach from the ...illage, by way of the car park and picnic ...te, runs along the side of a wood and ...ives a sudden close-up view of the castle. ...oodrich is now so surrounded by trees ...at, from a distance, it is visible only ...om the open country over the river and ...e old road to Ross-on-Wye, near Kerne ...ridge.

The path bends round the outside of ...e moat and crosses the rock-cut ditch ...und the barbican. Some early Christian ...urials have been found immediately ...longside the path.

...arbican

...he castle is roughly square in plan, with round towers at three of the corners and a round-fronted gatehouse at the fourth. In front of this main gatehouse is an extra defence in the form of a D-shaped barbican (compare the illustrations on pages 5 and 20) with its own separate ditch and gates. Only the lower parts of the walls remain, with a stone bench running round the inside, probably for the convenience of people waiting their turn to be admitted into the castle.

A barbican (from the Arabic *bab-khanah*, a gatehouse) usually means an outwork protecting a gateway. There are early thirteenth-century barbicans outside the entrances to Dover Castle and Pembroke Castle. It is not known when the Goodrich barbican was built, but two very similar D-shaped enclosures were built in the 1270s at the Tower of London

3

17 Keep

8 Inner ward

9 Chapel

24 Steps to basement below solar

21 High end of great hall

29 Remains of stairs between southwest tower and stables

18 Kitchen

19 Angle of curtain wall

Rock foundation

Some of the features numbered in the Tour of the Castle (pages 3-17) cannot b this aerial view. Refer to the plan on the centre pages

11 Rooms over chapel
and gate passage

4 Site of
drawbridge

2 Stepped ramp
to gatehouse

3 Site of
guardchamber

Barbican

1 Wooden
bridge across
outer moat

27 Arches
under site of
drawbridge

12 Wall walk

Dry moat

SKYSCAN

Chapel tower and east wall walk seen from the inner ward. In good light the lines of former roofs of the east range can be made out against the walls of chapel tower

and at Sandal near Wakefield in Yorkshire.

The wooden bridge (**1** on the illustration on pages 4-5 and the plan on the centre pages) across the outer moat, which could not be filled with water, is a modern replica; the side walls of the entrance gateway can be seen at the inner end. The first part of the stepped ramp **2** to the gatehouse is based on a solid medieval arch and was protected by a guardchamber **3** on the right, which also watched the steps to the outer ward.

The ramp is a good point from which to look at the defensive ditches. The main ditch is 90 feet wide and 28 feet deep (27 by 8m) and is cut into the natural red sandstone rock, forming a very convenient quarry for the stone that was used to build much of the castle. The ditch was

necessary on only two sides of the castle: elsewhere the steep slope down to the river and another forming a lateral valley were defence enough. The top of the ramp originally had a gap with a drawbridge **4** which could be drawn up when necessary; the holes on which it pivoted can be seen low down.

Gate passage

As you go up the entrance ramp, notice that the towers on either side of the passage are unequal in size. That on the left has a large fifteenth-century window to light the chapel. Like all the other towers, this one has tall pyramidal spurs so that it tapers upwards from a square base to a round top. This feature can be

een in several other castles nearby; it not
nly made the tower more rigid against
ttempts to undermine it but also helped
o deflect missiles launched against the
ower. The gatehouse on the right
ontained the porter's lodge, controlling
ccess to the gate passage.

Look at the walls of the gate passage **5**
nd the stone-vaulted roof above your
ead. The narrow vertical slots are where
ne portcullis was raised and lowered; this
as a wooden grill bound with iron which
as an added protection to prevent the
astle doors from being forced open by
ttackers. The 'murder holes'
neurtrières) in the vault above your head
ould allow the defenders to shoot down
r drop missiles on attackers' heads or to
ut out fires lit in front of the doors.

Turn right halfway along into a narrow
passage. This leads (left) to a latrine
within the wall **6** and (right) to the vaulted
porters' lodge **7** with a hooded fireplace
and slit windows which look out in three
directions: into the gate passage, to the
entrance ramp and over the outer ward
and river.

Chapel

Return to the gate passage, go through to
the inner ward (courtyard or bailey) **8** and
turn left and immediately left again into
the chapel **9**. This contains features of
several dates: the large trefoil-headed
'decorated' windows at either end date
from the fifteenth century, as do the
projecting corbel stones (carved with

*nterior of the chapel showing the fifteenth-century east window with restored tracery, a sedile
priest's seat), piscinas (basins), and carved stone corbels*

angels holding shields) and the ornamental drain recesses (piscinas) in both side walls. The staircase on the left (note the narrow window looking into the gate passage) and the upper doorways were also added when a wooden gallery was put in, with another building outside linking the gatehouse with the guest hall (see page 21).

At the far end is the base of the altar, with a cupboard (aumbry) on the left and a thirteenth-century priest's seat recess (sedile) on the right. In the window recess to the right there are some faint traces of painted decoration in the plaster. The window in the recess nearer the entrance is artfully angled round so that it gains light from outside the castle. This recess also has a cupboard.

Radar window
The window in the west wall, by the entrance to the chapel, commemorates the personnel of the Radar Research Squadron and, in particular, the tragedy of 7 June 1942, when a Halifax aircraft

Radar window in the west wall of the chapel

carrying the prototype bombing-aid radar crashed near Goodrich Castle, killing all eleven people on board.

The principle of RAdio Detection And Ranging (RADAR), the measurement of the range and direction of objects by their reflection of electromagnetic waves, was developed in Britain from 1935 as a defence against enemy ships and aircraft. The Radar Research Squadron was formed to develop the application of the principle as an aid to navigation.

Chapel tower and gatehouse
On leaving the chapel turn left again. To reach the basement below, go past the spiral staircase and down the straight flight of steps **10**.

Next, climb the spiral staircase **11** to the rooms over the chapel and gate passage. Note the back-to-back fireplaces, making these a pair of comfortable rooms. There is a fine view over the River Wye.

In the floor are slots for the two portcullises and the murder holes above the entrance passage. The recesses in the far wall provided space for the counterweights for the portcullis, and in the side wall you can trace the pivot hole for the roller round which the ropes for raising and lowering it were wound.

East wall walk
and southeast tower
Return to the top of the spiral staircase and turn left along the passage leading on to the wall walk **12**. Note the large cross-shaped arrowloops in the parapet wall. This is a good place from which to observe the layout of the castle, bettered only by the view from the top of the keep.

The square keep (of lighter coloured stone) was flanked by three ranges: one immediately below you on the wall walk, another on the opposite side of the inner

!ast range, wall walk and southeast tower, with the entrance to the dungeon between the foot of !he steps and the modern entrance to the keep

vard, and a third to the right. These were inked by narrow covered alleyways marked by the modern paths).

Pass into the first-floor level of the outheast tower. This tower was for domestic use as a residence on three loors; there are window openings with eats and large hooded fireplaces. To your ight are the remains of a spiral staircase going to the upper floor, but our route oes down a long flight of steps **13**, urning right down to the basement, vhere you can see the bare rock oundations on the right **14**.

East range

Returning to the inner ward and looking cross to the gatehouse and chapel tower, marks on the wall give clues about how his range of buildings developed (see the llustration on page 6).

The thirteenth-century building may

have been only stables, or storage at the level of the chapel basement. Its roofline is marked by the projecting horizontal stringcourse and recess for a timber wall-plate in the wall on the right. The second phase had the ground raised to the present level, a new sloping roof extending upwards over the wall walk and parapet, with new windows. Eventually (probably in the fifteenth century) a pitched roof was erected even higher, and two upper floors were put in, reached from doorways in the spiral staircase turret and with a new fireplace for heating. Vestiges of this can be seen in the chapel wall.

This range, with its large latrine block **15**, was designed for communal living by the castle staff and garrison.

Prison

The narrow doorway **16** to the left of the keep leads down into a dark narrow prison

The twelfth-century keep. The original entrance (now a window above the present doorway) was at first-floor level, reached by external stairs. The steps on the left lead to the wall walk by the southeast tower, and the doorway to the left of the keep leads to the dungeon. The steps on the right of the picture led from the great hall to the top floor of the southwest tower

View from the top of the keep, with the great hall, northwest tower and solar on the left and the gatehouse and chapel tower on the right of the inner ward

with a vaulted roof. Notice the square holes outside the stone doorframe; these held a wooden bar which could be slid across in front of the door to prevent it from being opened. Normally barholes are on the inside of a doorframe to keep people out, but of course here the door was to keep people in.

Keep

Continuing clockwise round the inner ward, the square tower next to the prison is the keep or donjon **17**, the earliest part of the castle remaining.

'Donjon' is the term for the main tower of a medieval castle. When such towers were no longer used by the castle lord to live in, they often became prisons because of the innate strength, hence 'dungeon.' At Goodrich the prison is alongside the keep. (See *Castle Keeps* on page 25.)

The keep was built in the twelfth century, not of local stone but of grey conglomerate, probably brought by river from the Forest of Dean, a few miles south of Goodrich. The stones are carefully cut square and laid in level courses (ashlar) with pilaster buttresses running up each wall and a projecting horizontal stringcourse decorated with chevrons. Above this level, in the north and west sides, are two round-topped Norman windows with columns on each side. A third opening, high on the east side, is later and was linked by a bridge to the southeast tower which you have just left.

The original entrance to the keep was at first-floor level (above the present entrance). It is now blocked up apart from a twin-light fifteenth-century window with decorated top. That entrance must originally have been reached by a timber staircase or a ladder. The present entrance at ground level is through a later doorway.

Inside, notice the upper floor levels marked by an offset of the wall and by projecting corbel stones at right angles, showing that the floor joists ran in different directions, so spreading the load evenly on the four walls. From the top of the modern wooden stairs, the opening through the wall may have been for a latrine or perhaps more likely to the upper floor of a timber hall, now gone. A narrow spiral staircase goes up to the modern roof.

From the roof there is a panoramic view. Sloping stones built into the walls here may indicate the pitch of an older roof ridge, but the proportions of the tower, and the lack of any evidence for the wall narrowing for a parapet, suggest that originally the tower may have risen at least another storey.

Kitchen

After leaving the keep, turn left round the corner of the tower. This space **18**, with its fireplaces, ovens and wall drain, was the late medieval kitchen area. The castle curtain wall projects at an angle here **19** instead of being straight; it may follow the line of an earlier smaller castle enclosure round the keep tower.

Southwest tower

Turn left on leaving the kitchen and enter the great hall. Turn left again and descend a flight of steps **20** into the basement of

Embrasure, with a relieving arch above it, in the basement of southwest tower

the southwest tower. There were two floors above the basement. The foundations of an earlier tower, which was also circular but of a smaller diameter than the existing building, can be traced on the floor of the basement. In the fifteenth century one of the two embrasures (narrow vertical slits) lighting this room was converted into a doorway (now blocked) to stairs leading down to the stables. Remains of the stairs are visible on the outside **29**.

The ground floor of this tower was entered by a double doorway from the screens passage, behind the timber screens in the great hall. This room was the buttery, where liquor, especially ale, was stored and issued.

In the north wall (above the doorway from the great hall) the doorway to a passage leading to a latrine can be seen.

Great hall

The great hall had three large windows in the outer wall, two to the left of a big fireplace recess and one on the right (the latter no longer remains). Above the window on the left is a doorway that led from the southwest tower to the wall walk.

The projecting stones (corbels) and vertical slots above the windows show where the roof brackets were originally fixed. An old description mentions one roof beam of oak 66 feet (20m) long and 2 feet (60cm) square. The 'high' end of the hall **21** was where the castle lord, his family and guests sat.

Vestibule and private chapel

Above the vestibule **22** was a small private chapel. The piscina and sedile can be traced above the door to the great hall. This chapel was for the use of the lord and his family; the garrison would have used the larger chapel.

Solar and northwest tower

Beyond the vestibule is the castle well **23**, which is 168 feet (51m) deep. From beside the well you can see into the solar (the lord's private room). The floor level (not much lower than the ground on which you are standing) can be traced where the side walls are offset.

Little remains of the northwest tower; the internal arrangements may not have differed greatly from those of the southeast and southwest towers. The tower is separated from the solar by two pointed arches, originally containing screens, which spring from a central column (see page 16).

There are large windows in the outer wall of the solar, like those in the great hall. A flat roof was replaced when a third floor level was inserted.

Go down the steps **24** to the basement below the solar. In the southeast corner **25** is a recess with a sink which was linked to the well by a pipe.

In the opposite wall is a small postern or sally port (external doorway). This was protected by double doors and a portcullis which could be lowered in the grooves on either side. Steps lead down to the outer ward **26**.

Outer ward

This ward (courtyard or bailey) runs round the edges of the natural slope, partly levelled off, with an outer and lower curtain wall with smaller turrets at the corners. Walk clockwise round the castle, turning right outside the postern.

Straight ahead is the wall of the barbican **3**. Turn right before reaching it and pass under the entrance ramp through either arch **27**: that on the left is a complete pointed arch with ribs, but the other is a half arch partly blocked. Looking up here you can see the blocking of the drawbridge pit and the openings through which its counterpoises could drop.

Above the rocky slope, beyond the arches, is the chapel tower with its big window, then the curtain wall, heightened when the domestic east range was adapted (page 21) and then the projecting latrine block **15**.

Take care descending the rocky slope to the grassy bed of the dry moat **28**. If is is wet you are advised to retrace your steps and go round the outside of the castle in the other direction.

Beyond the southeast tower is the projecting angle of the curtain wall **19**, built on solid rock, with the lighter coloured Norman keep towering above it.

Round the next corner, beyond the southwest tower, are the foundations of the stables, stone paved with drain channels. Traces remain of stairs **29** in the southwest tower; these gave access between the castle and the stables. Beyond the northwest tower you arrive

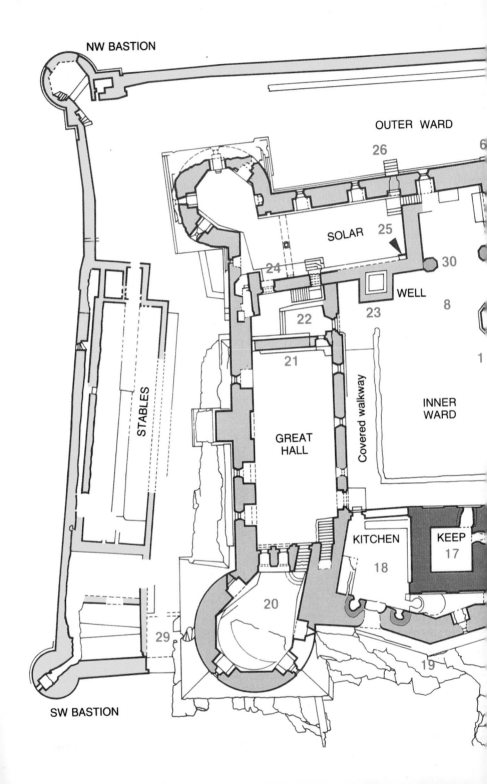

NW BASTION

OUTER WARD

26 6

SOLAR 25

30

24

WELL

22 23 8

21 1

STABLES

GREAT
HALL

Covered walkway

INNER
WARD

KITCHEN 18 KEEP 17

20

29 19

SW BASTION

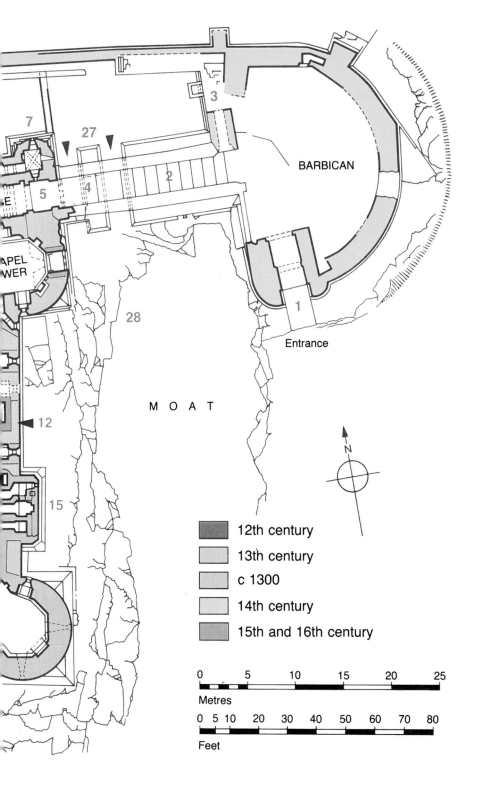

7

27

3

BARBICAN

2

5

4

E

APEL
WER

1

28

Entrance

12

M O A T

N

15

	12th century
	13th century
	c 1300
	14th century
	15th and 16th century

0   5   10   15   20   25

Metres

0 5 10   20   30   40   50   60   70   80

Feet

The solar, private chamber, with the remains of the northwest tower beyond it. The solar was at the same level as the inner ward. Wooden screens, either side of the central column, divided the building. A sally port on the outer wall of the room below leads to the outer ward

Southwest tower with the keep and the southeast tower to the right. At the foot of the southwest tower are remains of stairs that connected it with the stables

...ack at the postern and can climb up to the inner ward.

As you return to the gatehouse, notice the octagonal foundation stones **30** of a late medieval building fitted in between the gatehouse and the solar.

An excellent *picnic site* and an *information point* and WC are by the car park. If you have enough time, a walk through the village to the river bank is described on the next page.

The *parish church*, which is as old as the castle, can be reached by a footpath from just beyond the village school. This leads across the school playing field, through a gate and diagonally up a sometimes rather overgrown slope to another gate and the churchyard.

River Wye Walks

Goodrich Castle and the River Wye, from a painting by A R Quinton

Goodrich Castle overlooks a long-distance footpath which follows the bank of the River Wye for many miles. A circular wall, beginning and ending at the castle car park, and including the spectacular viewpoint of the Symonds Yat rock, follows a great loop in the river. It is, however, a fairly long walk (a little over 8 miles) and takes 4 hours or longer to complete. Clear directions, with a good map and illustrations, are given in the *Pathfinder Guide to Wye Valley and Forest of Dean Walks* which is published by Ordnance Survey/Jarrold. Alternatively, walks can be planned with *Outdoor Leisure map 14* or *Landranger map 162*.

A shorter walk to Kerne Bridge and

back (some 2 miles) takes about 1 hour. On leaving the castle, go beyond the car park as far as the crossroads. Turn sharp left towards Welsh Bicknor. After about 100 yards you cross a road bridge. Immediately turn left down some steep steps.

The farm on your left occupies the site of Flanesford Priory. A licence to build a chantry chapel 'in the liberty of the castle of Goodrich' was issued to Sir Richard Talbot in 1338 but in 1346 the chantry lands were assigned to a new Augustinian priory. After the Dissolution of the Monasteries, the priory and its lands were assigned to the Earl of Shrewsbury on condition that a chantry chapel was built there to pray for the King's soul. The farmyard occupies the site of the priory cloister, and the buildings nearest the road are believed to be the old dining hall for the monks.

Continue downhill towards the river. At Kerne Bridge (built in 1828) you can turn right along the river before or after crossing the bridge. If you do not cross the river, but climb over the stile and go down the steps to the riverside path, you can extend the walk along the riverbank to another path which leads back over the ridge to the village.

Around here you may see traces of the track of the railway that once followed and twice crossed the River Wye, and bored through the hills on two sharp bends in the river (one at Symonds Yat), on its way from Ross to Monmouth. Sadly this scenic line was axed by Dr Beeching in the early 1960s.

View over the River Wye from the top of Goodrich Castle keep

History of Goodrich

Goodrich castle as it may have been in its heyday

Goodrich and the River Wye

The castle looks out over a crossing point of the river which was used for many centuries. The Roman Road between Ariconium (near Weston under Penyard) and Blestium (Monmouth) passed this way. Its line is probably marked by the old lanes converging on the river a little upstream of the castle, just to the left of the woods on the far bank. The village of Walford across the river takes its name from Welsh ford. The area was only taken from the Welsh by the Normans in the late eleventh century. Recently a number of early Christian burials were found just outside the castle moat.

The old road continued in use. Henry Bolingbroke, later Henry IV, is said to have given the rights of the ferry to the boatman who first told him of the birth of his son (later Henry V) in Monmouth as he crossed the Wye here in 1388. To cross, the boatman hauled on a rope suspended over the river. Similar ferries are still used for crossing the Wye near Symonds Yat, although Kerne Bridge was built in the early nineteenth century.

Norman castle

Goodrich Castle is mentioned first in a document dated 1101-02. Godric Mappeston held Hulle (Howle, 2 miles east of Goodrich) at the time of the Domesday Book (1086) and a note in a twelfth-century copy of part of the Domesday Book connects the castle with Godric. It is not known what the original castle looked like, but it probably was a simple enclosure of bank and ditch with a timber palisade and watch tower.

The stone tower was probably built as a replacement a generation later, during the war between King Stephen and the Empress Matilda (daughter of King Henry I) from 1138 to 1153, when the area was disputed between the Earls of Gloucester and Hereford. Goodrich was part of the estates of Gilbert Fitz Gilbert de Clare, (created Earl of Pembroke in 1138) but returned to royal ownership in 1176. Throughout the twelfth century 'Castellum Godrici' remained just a place name and there are no records of the building or occupation of the castle itself.

Thirteenth-century rebuilding

The first proper mention of the castle was in 1204, when King John gave it to William Marshal on his marriage to the heiress of the earldom of Pembroke. Pembroke was the medieval route to Ireland, and the earls had great estates there after the Norman Conquest in the late twelfth century. William had risen from humble origins because of his support for four kings: Henry II, Richard I, John and finally Henry III.

It was probably at this time that the first stone walls and towers were built around the old keep, just as Marshal was doing at Chepstow Castle, near the Wye estuary, and as other Marcher lords did at their castles along the border between England and Wales.

William Marshal's fourth son died childless in the keep at Goodrich Castle in 1245, and the castle and earldom passed through his niece Joan to her husband, William de Valence, half brother of King Henry III, who held it for nearly fifty years. Grants of oak trees from royal forests in 1280 and 1282, and the presence of royal clerks and workmen

nearby early in 1296, suggest that major rebuilding work was taking place here during the reign of Edward I. The style of the gatehouse and barbican and the spurs in the drum towers, support this.

Domestic planning

The old keep (and perhaps a timber hall alongside) were downgraded about 1300 to create a prison and strongroom, and a kitchen area. Three separate ranges were built on the other three sides of the courtyard, each consisting of a hall with a three-storeyed residential tower at the end. Each represented a different standard of accommodation; the best was to the west, with its gallery and vestibule, forming the castle owners' suite and setting for display banquets.

By contrast the east wing was for communal living by the castle staff and garrison. The north range between them was intended for principal guests, but was later reorganised to link it with the gatehouse and main chapel, giving extra accommodation and increasing the limited facilities previously available to the constable commanding the castle from his small apartment over the gateway.

William de Valence

William was the fourth son of Hugh X, Count of La Marche, and of Isabella of Angoulême, the widow of King John of England. When the French royal house conquered the province of Poitou, William and two of his brothers came to England where they were given lands by their half brother, King Henry III. In 1247 William married the heiress of the Pembroke estates of the Marshal family.

A proud and violent man, William was exiled in 1258 in response to baronial pressure. He returned to support the King and was again exiled in 1264/5 during the

Kitchen utensils found during excavations at Goodrich Castle

baronial triumph. He took part in the Crusade of 1270-73 and was a royal councillor (especially for Aquitaine). He built at least one other castle besides Goodrich, in Limousin in France. The magnificent tombs of himself and his son Aymer are in Westminster Abbey.

Countess of Pembroke's expenses at Goodrich Castle

William de Valence died in May 1296 leaving Goodrich to his wife Joan in dower. She lived here for long periods until she died in 1307. A manuscript record of her expenses for the year beginning 29 September 1296 survives and gives fascinating details of life in a baronial household 700 years ago. Much of the countess's regular needs would have been met in kind from one or other of her manors, round which she progressed (no doubt to collect dues and consume fresh produce) and would not be enrolled on the accounts.

Before wintering at Goodrich, the Countess's baker was sent ahead to prepare bread, well before the household arrived. Stores of pork, eggs, cheese and milk were already there, and mutton, beef and venison were purchased. The Countess travelled with at least five pack-horses and carts to carry her luggage (including her bed). She had her own carriage, and the Goodrich establishment included a large wagon which from time to time needed new harnesses and wheel repairs.

Guests included the de Clare family (Earls of Gloucester), Joan's son Aymer and her daughter Isabel, local lords and ladies and the heads of several religious houses, both male and female. Some remained for weeks at a time, and the accommodation within the castle must have been fully used. Twenty poor people were fed each day, the number rising to over sixty at Easter.

A pipe of wine (equivalent to about 700 modern bottles) was bought in Bristol and shipped to the castle at a total cost of under £4. Beer was bought at Monmouth and was also brewed at the castle, malt and oats being brought from the estate, and water was brought in to supplement the castle well supply. Wye salmon, then as now, were considered a delicacy, and were often given as a present to departing guests. A net was purchased at Abergavenny for the Wye fishermen, and servants were sent to Chepstow, Gloucester, Bristol and even Southampton to buy fish (particularly eels, hake and herring). Large quantities of wood for fuel were cut from the Dowards (the hills opposite Symonds Yat) as well as Bishops Wood across the river, and sixty horses were hired to bring it down to the boat.

A messenger took ten days to get to

London and back. Others went to Ireland and Pembroke to deal with business on the countess's estates, which produced much of her income.

Of the countess herself, we read about the cost of the regular light in her own room, the purchase of rice and sugar 'for my lady's use,' a tailor going to Bristol for her new robes with red trimming, and of the buying of a pair of a pair of stockings (5 pence) and boots (18 pence). By May 1297, Joan de Valence, Countess of Pembroke, was off again on her summer progress from Goodrich Castle around her other estates.

The Talbots

William's son, Aymer de Valence, died in 1324 and the castle passed to his niece Elizabeth Comyn, who was forced to surrender her rights to Hugh Despencer. However, Elizabeth's husband, Richard Talbot, recovered the estates shortly afterwards and in 1346 they founded an Augustinian priory near the castle (see page 18) and later were permitted to have a prison for local malefactors in the castle.

The castle was a principal residence of the Talbots who were made richer by ransoms secured during the Hundred Years' War, and were created Earls of Shrewsbury in 1442. The priory was suppressed in 1538. By 1616 when the castle was sold to Henry Grey, Earl of Kent, it was disused.

Civil War (1642-48)

In 1643 the castle was occupied for Parliament by Captain Kyrle with 100 men. The Royalist vicar of Goodrich (Thomas Swift, grandfather of the author of *Gulliver's Travels*) had built a remarkable three-winged house nearby, which was pillaged five times by the Roundheads. In the last robbery, even the food and clothing of the vicar's children and servants were stolen.

At the end of the year the garrison was withdrawn, and when Hereford was reoccupied by Roundheads in 1645 the Royalists withdrew to Goodrich Castle under the leadership of Sir Henry Lingen.

In March 1646 a surprise attack by Colonel Birch led to the capture of the sixteen-man guard at the ferry and of eighty horses in the castle stables which were set on fire. The siege was desultory at first, with occasional raids and some

Horse shoes and parts of bridles, stirrups, a bit and curry comb found during excavations at Goodrich Castle

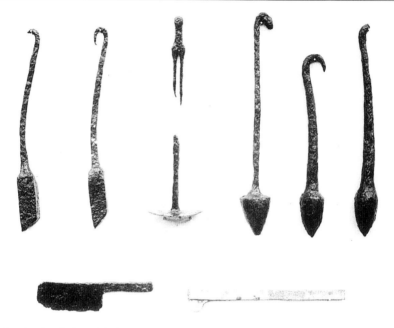

Set of plumbers' tools found during excavations at Goodrich Castle

small-scale hand-to-hand fighting, but by June 1646 mining of the weakened river side of the castle was begun and Colonel Birch had a mortar cast which was capable of throwing a 200 pound (85kg) shot.

The 104-man garrison surrendered, no doubt influenced both by the imminence of the explosion of the mine under the walls and by the surrender of King Charles I. They were down to their last few barrels of powder but had good stores of corn and meal, butter, cheese and beef, sixty flitches of bacon, thirty barrels of beer and hogsheads of claret and sack (sherry).

To prevent its continued defensive use, the castle was partly demolished and the main timbers and lead roofs taken away. The Countess of Kent was awarded £1000 in compensation for the demolition.

Later history

Admiral Thomas Griffin bought the castle ruins on the death of the Duke of Kent in 1740; the title Viscount Goodrich remained with the Grey family. In 1828 Edward Blore, the architect, commenced building a great towered house northwest of the castle for Sir Samuel Rush Meyrick to display his collection of old armour. The house was demolished in the 1960s but the twin-towered gatehouse is still a landmark on the road to Ross-on-Wye.

An account of a party visit to the castle ruins in the 1890s mentions an ash tree with a 12 foot (3.6m) girth, growing in the courtyard and the visitors gathering wild roses from the top of the keep. As late as 1925 the site was very overgrown but its guardians, the Commissioners of Works, commenced repairs and clearance to conserve and display the castle, work being continued by English Heritage.

Much bigger than that at Goodrich, Rochester Castle keep is one of the finest surviving Norman keeps. One corner had to be rebuilt after it was undermined and brought down during the siege of 1215. This picture shows the steps round one corner of the keep and through the forebuilding to the entrance at first-floor level

The keep (great tower or donjon) was a defensive innovation. Its origin is uncertain - towers go back a long way - but the keep flourished particularly in eleventh- and twelfth-century England and Normandy. Until then, lordly residences had usually consisted of several buildings loosely linked with rudimentary defences.

Soon after 1066 the White Tower of London was built as a brilliant compression of a palace (public hall, rooms for sleeping and eating, and chapels) into a single block several storeys high, with thick walls to carry the floor load and protect against attack.

Apart from the chapels, the White Tower design became fairly typical, but with added emphasis being given to height. This not only improved the all-round view, but such a towering mass of masonry was an unspoken warning, a

King John leading an attack on Rochester castle during the siege of 1215

VICTOR AMBRUS

symbol of domination of its lord (king or wealthy landowner) over others.

Inside the keep, the ground floor or basement was for storage, with only tiny openings for shooting through, ventilation and light. The public hall was on the floor above, reached by permanent or temporary stairs to restrict access. The upper floors (reached by ladders or wall stairs, often spiralling up in an angle) were for private rooms, often lit by fair-sized windows high above the ground. The walls were carried up to a crenellated parapet high above the roof, to protect it from fire-arrows.

Keeps were usually intended for independent defence, and traces of the necessary fireplaces, wellshafts and latrines can often be found. As everything (and everybody) had to pass up and down the entrance stairs, these were often enclosed in a forebuilding.

Increasing needs for privacy led to rooms in corner turrets and experiments with other layouts. Polygonal and round keeps were erected in the late twelfth century, but the development of powerful high trajectory weapons (particularly the trebuchet) and better longbows and crossbows, meant that attackers had to be kept at a greater distance from the defences than before. Consequently defences stopped being focused on a central great tower and passed to concentric rings of walls with towers at intervals designed for active, not passive, defence.

These developments were very expensive, and more economical square keeps continued to be built, particularly on the Welsh and Scottish borders, throughout the Middle Ages. As long as supplies of food and water lasted, the defenders were in a very strong position. At Rochester, in 1215, the garrison held out long after one corner of the keep had been undermined and collapsed, exposing all five floors.

Goodrich is a very small keep, indeed its thick walls take up two-thirds of its total area.

Sieges

A siege is a method of warfare by which an attacker intends to force the defenders of a castle (or even a city or country) to surrender by denying them supplies of food and water and means of defence. Given an adequate force of besiegers, surrender will eventually be inevitable because of starvation or demoralisation. Matters were often speeded up by active attack on the object.

A castle presents a series of obstacles for an attacker to overcome, culminating in the passive mass of the central tower. Surrounding this was a series of walls of timber or stone (with towers projecting to make it easier to defend the base of the walls) often standing on high earth banks that were built up when digging external ditches, so doubling the defensive potential.

The common method of attack was to attempt to fill in the ditch and bring mobile towers or ladders up to the castle walls with the intention of gaining a foothold on the wall top (where the defenders would be concentrated), getting inside and opening a gate for a mass invasion. If this proved impossible, the walls might be attacked directly with picks or battering rams, or a tunnel be excavated beneath the wall, which would be undermined and collapse.

Stone-throwing engines (later guns) were used either to break the walls directly or to throw projectiles on to the roofs of the castle buildings and make them uninhabitable. Projectiles consisted of anything available - rubbish and dead animals were used as an early form of germ warfare.